A souvenir guide

Carding Mill Valley and the Long Mynd
Shropshire

Andrew Fusek Peters

A Moving Landscape	2
So much to explore	4
Man on the Mynd	6
Wealth in wool	8
How the valley got its name	10
After sheep, tourists	12
A change in management	14
The modern-day Mynd	16
Something for Everyone	18
The ponies of the Mynd	19
Outdoor play	20
For nature lovers	22
The birds of the Mynd	24
The Mynd in all seasons	26
Best for bird-spotting	28
Getting starry-eyed	30
What the Mynd means to me	32

National Trust

A Moving Landscape

Long Mynd derives from the Welsh for 'Long Mountain'. As this giant slumbers in the Shropshire Hills, sometimes under a blanket of purple heather, it's hard to imagine a time before it existed, as it has been millennia in the making.

Between 570 and 550 million years ago, muds, sands and gravels washed into a shallow sea near the Antarctic Circle. They were compressed over aeons of time to form mudstones, sandstones and conglomerates, and then folded and tilted to form the layered rocks of the Long Mynd. The shifting of tectonic plates meant the Mynd moved here at the stately pace of three centimetres a year. Later, Ice Age glaciers melted and the meltwater cut the steep-sided valleys known as 'batches'.

A brief history

As the ice retreated, humans moved north. The Portway became a main trading route and trees were cleared. These people built settlements on top of the hill, because visibility made them safer, and it was easier to clear the willows and birches that grew there compared to the larger trees in the valleys.

After the Norman Conquest the feudal system was imposed. Abbeys owned vast swathes of land and also controlled the lucrative wool trade. But the Mynd was always set aside for commoners to graze their animals and gather wood. These rights co-existed later on with the rise of shooting and the management of the Mynd as a grouse moor. When the railways came in the 19th century, Church Stretton marketed itself as 'Little Switzerland'. Tourism, as we know it, was born and many came to sample the delights of the Mynd.

When the National Trust bought the Mynd in 1965, the land was heavily grazed and in poor health. A huge amount of restoration work continues to be carried out to make the Mynd accessible to walkers, cyclists, students, photographers and watchers of wildlife, who all enjoy one of the great jewels in the Shropshire landscape.

Left The Long Mynd at dawn

So much to explore

The Long Mynd offers both nature and history in abundance, and there is, literally and metaphorically, a lot of ground to cover. This guidebook will take you to some of the Mynd's less explored corners and share with you some of its stories along the way.

The Long Mynd is the National Trust's biggest outdoor education centre, with 30,000 students visiting each year. They come to study some of the oldest rocks in the world. For many, this is their first countryside visit.

Experienced National Trust education staff show how volcanic activity, the effects of tectonic plates and glaciers, erosion, grazing and conservation management have made the Mynd what it is today.

Life through a lens
Students also spend time understanding adaptation and evolution via the incredibly clean streams that run through the valleys. Many look at the mayfly larvae, which are specially flattened, enabling them to live under stones on the stream bed without being washed away. Pond-dipping and the use of hand lenses or microscopes in the onsite field studies laboratory help young people identify species and appreciate their diversity.

Above left Scanning the clear waters of Carding Mill Valley for wildlife

Left A golden-ringed dragonfly laying her eggs

Above Walkers approaching the slopes of Burway Hill

Darwin's predictions

On the subject of proving the existence of primordial lifeforms, Charles Darwin wrote in *The Origin of Species* (1859) that 'Traces of life have been detected in the Longmynd beds'. In this ancient landscape people have continued to search for evidence of prehistoric life. Up above the Carding Mill Valley reservoir, there is a section of rock face that has been caged off to protect it from the more intrepid fossil hunters. The rocks bear tiny indentations that were made in shallow water muds and subsequently preserved. Some of these, astonishingly, are fossilised rain prints; others, just as remarkably, have been found to be impressions of microbiological life forms – bacteria and algae – that colonised a muddy shoreline 570 million years ago. Proof of Darwin's ideas that the Long Mynd has been long inhabited, and proof that it has been raining on the Long Mynd for a long time!

Man on the Mynd

After the seismic events that
brought the Mynd to its current
position, the next biggest influence
and shaper of the landscape was
the activity of man.

When the glaciers retreated, Neolithic traders created and used the ancient Portway to avoid the forested and boggy valleys. Elevation gave warning of potential danger from attackers and the ridgeway was always firmer underfoot. Stone axes were used to clear the upland areas of trees. One such axe was discovered on the Mynd in the 19th century. Fire was used to keep the Mynd open and viable for grazing stock. By the mid- to late Bronze Age, the Mynd was deforested. There are many old burial mounds dotted along the Portway. Cross-ridge dykes show evidence of barriers put across trackways in a landscape that was tightly controlled and managed, perhaps in an early form of toll-crossing.

Shaping the landscape

Grazing continued as a vital means of subsistence after the Norman Conquest, when the manor-based feudal system was introduced. The lord of the manor protected serfs and villeins in return for their labour. Protection mainly took the form of common rights to graze and gather resources and fuel from the poorest-quality lands, called the waste of the manor, in exchange for a share of the harvest. The best fields in the valleys were reserved for the lord of the manor, but the Mynd stayed as an unenclosed common. This common land and the rights that derived from it kept many commoners alive and went on to shape much of the Mynd we see today.

As more and more land was enclosed in the 18th and 19th centuries, the commoners of Church Stretton had to fight to protect their rights. But this period also saw a rise in the popularity of grouse shooting and it made sense for the owners to keep the Mynd open and unfenced.

Sheep in the landscape

By the time the Mynd was bought in 1965 by the National Trust, the landscape was over-grazed and many of the paths and trackways were in poor repair due to the large number of visitors and illegal vehicle use. Backed by government grants, a reduction in the number of sheep was negotiated with the commoners, and as grazing was reduced, the heather came back. With it, many species of wildlife increased. Grayling butterfly and red grouse are notably more numerous, with up to 70 pairs of the latter counted on the Mynd in recent years.

Where burning was originally used to keep the top of the Mynd clear, it is now a vital part of the National Trust's work. Heather and gorse are targeted in controlled burning during March and October. Heather is burned to aid regeneration and encourage flowering, and gorse is cleared in this way to help the movement of sheep.

ON THE "WIMBERRY HILL," LONGMYND.   Photo by E. S. Cobbold.

Left Iron Age men brought animals to graze the Mynd

Above left Bodbury hillfort

Above Bilberries were once a product of the hill, their juice used for dyeing wool and cotton

Wealth in wool

As we've already seen, man made the Mynd what it is today, but there is another species whose presence has had a profound impact. More than the act of grazing, it was the way in which sheep were allowed to roam all over the Mynd, unbarred by hedges and fences, that has had the largest effect on today's landscape.

Wool was the oil of the Middle Ages, traded with European cloth manufacturers from long-established markets such as Church Stretton. Once wool became a valued commodity, it was not just commoners who grazed their flocks on the Mynd without need for payment. The abbeys, and later the manorial lords, used this upland for massive profit. It helped that the indigenous, or 'Longmynd', sheep had the most prized fleeces in the country. Sadly, they are now extinct.

In 1175, Henry II granted Haughmond Abbey rights of grazing on the Mynd for both sheep and horses. These huge flocks quickly helped Shropshire wool merchants to become the richest in England. A weekly market began in Church Stretton in 1214 and many of the tracks we now use across the Mynd were created by local people with ponies carrying goods to the nearest market. The Burway, which is the main route onto the Mynd from Church Stretton, started life as an ancient packhorse route.

This wealth of wool benefitted both the church and, after the Dissolution of the Monasteries in the 1530s, entrepreneurial wool merchants. Nearby Stokesay Castle is a classic example, where wool money financed the addition of crenellations to its walls. Such battlements were not necessary for defence, but they made a very expensive status and fashion statement.

Commoners' rights

In the late 18th century, most landowners tried to seize and enclose traditional commons, but the commoners fought for and held on to their rights, with the Church Stretton Commoners' Association set up in 1868 to combat this encroachment.

Commoners had to continuously defend their rights against landowners and their ideas of how the Mynd should be managed. When grouse hunting became a popular sport amongst the gentry in the 19th century, the lord of the Long

Top It is the grazing of sheep by commoners that has created and helped to preserve the distinctive landscape of the Long Mynd

Above A shepherd photographed on the Long Mynd near the Boiling Well

Mynd manor wanted to ban grazing cattle, because they damaged the butts – hides screened by turf walls used for grouse hunting. Names such as Cow Ridge, Calf Ridge and Bullocksmoor pre-dated by centuries the formal banning of cattle in 1908.

Managing the Mynd

The changing climate and patterns of human movement, the vagaries of the feudal lord–serf relationship, the way man has manipulated his environment for commercial gain and recreational pursuits, all these have gone into shaping the Long Mynd. It's a unique combination of events that leaves us a unique landscape.

    Thanks to humble sheep and ancient rights, the National Trust, in the role of guardian,

though legally still the lord of the manor, now manages a picturesque and wildlife-friendly landscape. A battle against fences has been won, leaving us with a rare and wide-open upland, which all can enjoy.

Below A red grouse hiding in the heather

How the valley got its name

If wool was the oil of the Middle Ages, mills were the refineries and factories. To achieve the highest prices, the raw product needed some processing and so the fleeces of the Longmynd sheep came here, to the mill in Carding Valley.

The Domesday Book tells us there was a mill at Stretton in 1086. This was most likely in what we now know as Carding Mill Valley. Up to 1811, the mill on this site was used for grinding corn. But on 27 May 1811 a storm brought torrential rain and the wooden structure of the mill was swept away in the floodwaters.

A brand new three-storey mill was built on the site. This became the new carding mill. The wheel had a diameter of 16 feet and was fed by leats (artificial watercourses) from a series of mill pools further up the valley. The upper car park is the site of one of the original mill pools, built to supply a good head of water to power the mill further down the valley. In the early part of the last century, it was used as an outdoor bathing pool with a wonderful view. In the winter, it made the perfect skating rink. A 'Depth – 3ft' sign still looks over the car park.

Above right **The buildings at Carding Mill Valley; the identity of the gentleman in the foreground is unknown**

Right **The mill pool in use as a bathing pool; it's now a car park**

BATHING POOL. CHURCH STRETTON

What is carding?

Carding is effectively combing the wool, removing impurities whilst forming long, continuous strands of wool called 'slivers'; the impurities were called 'slubs'. At first, the combing was done in homes by people using teasels, a kind of thistle. One type of thistle belongs to the *Carduus* genus, and so the process became known as carding. By striking the wool with bunches of teasels, the wool could be 'teased' straight. Later, spiked paddles rather like table-tennis bats with wire teeth were used. Later still, or more accurately after 1775, when inventor and industrialist Sir Richard Arkwright patented his carding engine, this ages-old occupation became mechanised and water-powered mills such as ours opened all over the country.

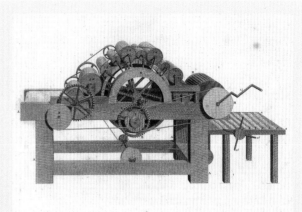

Working the wool

The mill was built to card wool, that is, to comb out the tangle of fibres from a fleece in order to form yarn. Rollers with spikes untangled the fibres ready for spinning, mainly by local women and children. In one hour the machinery could supply wool to local spinners and weavers that would have taken a week to card by hand.

The 1841 Census gives us the various job titles of those who worked at the mill: wool picker; sorter; the yarn slubber who took out the 'slubs' or imperfections in the yarn; carding engine feeder; spinner and flannel weaver. Many of the workers lived in the factory or adjoining cottages. Each July, Church Stretton held an annual wool market under the Market Hall in the High Street where fleeces were bought and sold and local workers brought their spun yarn.

Right The last photo taken of Carding Valley's mill

After sheep, tourists

The railway arrived in Church Stretton in 1852, and the Church Stretton Advancement Association decided to rebrand the Mynd as 'Little Switzerland' and Lightspout Waterfall, rather optimistically, as 'England's Little Niagara'.

As they do today, bank holidays brought thousands of visitors; unlike today, Victorian tourists arrived in specially booked trains. These visitors could then either walk or hire ponies, dogcarts or horse-drawn carriages.

'It is also a favourite place for picnics, and we had gone fully provided for an emergency of this latter description. With an appetite sharpened by our long ramble over the beautiful moorland, we seated ourselves joyfully on the bank partly surrounding a beautiful clear spring of water, the source of one of the many streams which water the gutters to the south east,' wrote Thomas Wright in *A Picnic on the Long Mynd*, in 1877.

Below The Victorian attractions of the Long Mynd

GREETINGS FROM CHURCH STRETTON

CARDING MILL VALLEY

THE LIGHTSPOUT

ASHES VALLEY. LITTLE STRETTON

CARDING MILL VALLEY & BATHING POOL

CARDING MILL VALLEY

New enterprises

The timing of this new source of income could not have been better, as the wool trade was in decline and another huge flood, in 1886, did great damage to the carding mill. The mill finally closed in 1904 and the old factory was converted into a hotel and café to cater to the new and growing tourist trade.

In 1920, a prefabricated wooden chalet was imported from Scandinavia and erected on site. The advert for the new Chalet Pavilion offered seating for 200 and 'quotations for Hot or Cold Luncheons, Teas &c, for Works-Outings, Private Parties, Choirs, Sunday Schools, &c, on application'. After the First World War, large open-topped vehicles called charabancs and greater numbers of motorcars began to clog up the roads.

During all this time the Mynd was still privately owned and used as a shooting moor for grouse, originally imported from the Yorkshire moors in the 1840s. By the 1930s, bags of a hundred brace from a single day's shoot were common. But overgrazing, encroaching bracken and too many visitors led to shooting's decline, until it was finally banned in 1990.

Tourism today

The National Trust was able to add to its Long Mynd property by buying the valley and these buildings in 1979. The Chalet Pavilion is now the Carding Mill Valley tea-room and shop, which serve delicious food, drinks and gifts all year round.

These days, the National Trust welcomes visitors in one valley in order to ease the pressure on the rest of the Mynd. This benefits wildlife and visitors, both of whom are free to seek quieter spots of the Mynd. There is a balance between welcoming tourists and maintaining and protecting one of our most important nature reserves and fragile eco-systems.

Above Tourists arriving by charabanc in the 1920s

Left From the 1950s visitors and vehicles increased dramatically

Below Still drawing the crowds today

A change in management

By 1965, when the Trust bought 1,820 hectares (4,500 acres) of the Long Mynd, the land was in poor condition. Over-grazing by sheep, compounded by the large number of visitors using, or rather not using, the inadequate parking facilities and paths meant more management was needed.

Under the Commons Registration Act, enacted in 1965, commoners were claiming the right to graze nearly 25,000 sheep, 150 cattle and over 1,000 ponies, an unsustainable level of grazing. So the Trust's first step on the path to change was a local campaign to raise the then huge sum of £18,500 so it could buy and enact the manorial rights of Stretton-en-le-Dale.

New controls

Some of the first works the Trust undertook were to fill in potholes, stop motorcycles roaming over the hill and begin to manage the visitor route.

It took until 1990 for the Trust to begin the process of renegotiating stock numbers with the commoners. An ecologist was employed to research the condition of the Mynd. The high stocking levels of animals on the Mynd were of primary concern, a result of European Union subsidy payments to hill farmers. The numbers were five and a half times the level that the heather on the common could cope with. Over the course of a few decades, grazing was destroying the ancient vegetation that came from centuries of the manorial system. It was also found that the heather was declining due to

the vast swathes of bracken covering the hill. Grouse numbers were down to 24 pairs and other indicator species, such as the emperor moth, were vanishing.

After coming to an agreement with the commoners in 2000, ewes were limited to 3,500 in the summer and 1,700 in the winter. These sheep, along with 30 ponies, graze an area that has now seen a remarkable recovery of bilberry, grass and heather.

Top left Heather is a favourite foodstuff of the brightly coloured emperor moth caterpillar

Top right As eye-catching when emerged, adult emperor moths are an indicator of healthy heathland

Above A grayling butterfly in the heather

A common hawker
dragonfly at a bog pool
by Pole Cottage

Returning wildlife

Alongside this recovery, trees are reappearing
and, if you are lucky, you might spot a cuckoo or
a tree pipit resting in one. Tussocks of grass are
attracting the grayling butterfly, wet boggy
flushes are filled with stonechat and whinchat.
The bog pools behind Pole Cottage, originally
dug out as shooting decoys, are now filled with
dragonflies, such as black darters and golden-
ringed dragonflies, and also reed buntings. The
heather itself is home to good numbers of
grouse and meadow pipit.

National Trust rangers and volunteers
manage invasive gorse and bracken, by cutting
and carrying out controlled burning each
October. They use a radio-controlled robot to
cut hillsides too steep to reach with traditional
methods. The battle is ongoing but determined.

The modern-day Mynd

Today the Mynd attracts thousands of visitors, who all find something to wonder at. But while we can feel refreshed and nourished by its beautiful scenery, we need to take care that the Mynd we visit today is the Mynd we'll have in the future.

The National Trust plays many different roles in its guardianship of the Mynd. Balanced grazing and the needs of the commoners cannot be addressed without keeping track of the bracken and gorse. If either gets out of control, the movement of sheep is hindered and the end result would be a tree-covered upland. There are a few conservationists who would argue for this, but the land up here has been open for thousands of years, and the flora and fauna have evolved for life in a heathland not a forest.

Visitors are of course welcomed but care is needed. There are small raised ridges that run along the roads that cross the Mynd. Before these were put in place, 4x4s would regularly go off road, with consequent damage to wildlife and habitat.

Walkers have an impact on the paths. Without intervention, many would become muddy and dangerous gullies. Hundreds of thousands of pounds have been spent using helicopters to bring in large stones for high-up paths, which are then set into the hills by the rangers with the help of a thousand volunteer days each year.

Enjoy responsibly

Dog owners are asked to keep their dogs under close control, especially with sheep around, and the majority are happy to enjoy the Mynd and treat wildlife and landscape with respect. (I am one of them.) But I have sadly seen an unleashed dog chase a sheep into a stream and have it grip it by the neck before its owner could intervene. The shock is often enough to kill a sheep.

A balance must be struck between the needs of sheep, wildlife and visitors. We have incredible migratory and resident bird species. From hobby to nesting peregrine, curlew to the wheatear, all are deserving of our care; else we might blink our eyes and see some of them gone by the next generation.

Above Expanses of heather-covered wilderness and deeply cut valleys and streams make for a complex ecosystem

Something for Everyone

Whether you walk, run, ride, cycle, photograph, stroll, glide, drive, study wildlife or dream of dark night skies, the Mynd is open all hours!

The ponies of the Mynd

For many, the ponies on the Mynd provide a wonderful backdrop to their visit. Today there are just 30 ponies (plus foals if under two years old), so seeing them makes a visit that much more memorable. Certainly the Mynd would not be the same without them.

Ponies have been bred here since the 12th century for use as packhorses along the Portway. The wild ponies you'll see on the Mynd today are from Welsh mountain pony stock, from a bloodline called Cwmdale Prefect. They are not tame but are looked after by one of the commoners, who checks on them regularly.

Apart from that, they live wild on the Mynd. They are reasonably approachable, but like any other wild animal, they are better regarded from a distance, so their gentle and sometimes playful natures can be observed and enjoyed. It goes without saying that dogs should be under control near the ponies and at all times.

If you're fortunate enough to see one of the 30 Long Mynd ponies, perhaps browsing the heather with their foals, you'll notice they are mostly grey or white, with each family group being of the same colour. The ponies are not only decorative; they serve a valuable function, their hooves helping to break up the bracken.

Left For those preferring an aerial view, paragliding is based at Asterton on the western side of the Mynd

Above Welsh mountain ponies on the Long Mynd

Outdoor play

The variety of activities on offer on the Mynd could leave you breathless. The choice is yours, but here are just some of my own recommendations and experiences of the Mynd.

During one September sunset, I drove up with my daughter to catch the last light off the western flanks of the Mynd. This was the perfect backdrop to shoot pictures for her blog. As I was photographing, a police car screeched to a halt in front of us and two officers leapt out, but only because the light was so arresting they had to capture the scene on their phones. There were still a few walkers about, and a posse of night cyclists with dipping headlights came over the path alongside the gliding station and headed off into the dusk.

This is where the Mynd excels. There are footpath routes for the intrepid as well as wheelchair-friendly meanders to great viewpoints; steep climbs for road cyclists and steep, twisty tracks for mountain bikers. If you ride, paraglide, glide, fly a model aeroplane, walk, talk, carry a picnic, thermos, raincoat, or even a swim suit for a dip in Carding Mill Valley reservoir, the Mynd has room for you. If you use your phone, tablet, or camera and are keen to capture wildlife and landscape, there are superb vistas and wonderful opportunities to be had throughout the seasons. Even if you just fancy a drive over the top and want to stop to look north to the Wrekin and beyond or west to the Stiperstones and Hay Bluff, then the Mynd will happily oblige come rain or shine.

For nature lovers

The Mynd may look like a wilderness, and indeed it is home to a fantastic array of wildlife, but the success of species depends on the health of their habitats. Under the care of the Trust, the grazing sheep and ponies now share the Mynd with flora and fauna flourishing like never before.

With good management and much work, the Mynd is now a flourishing upland. Degraded landscape has recovered and the great mix of heather and bilberry makes the perfect cover and habitat for many species. They are the equivalent of miniature forests playing the role of nesting sites, shelter and food provider. In particular, red grouse have done fantastically well, as they feed on heather. Interestingly, the fine grit on paths, such as the easy-access route to Pole Bank, is perfect for helping grouse digest tough fibres, so quiet dawn and dusk walkers are in with a chance of an encounter.

Bottom far left Cotton grass

Above Bog bean in Wildmoor Pool

Middle Heather at the edge of a bog pool

Below left A bilberry bumblebee on clover

Left A female skylark with worm

The heather also makes a great home for skylarks, numbers of which are declining in the UK. At last count, the Mynd supported 200 pairs. Meadow pipits are the commonest small brown bird on the hill. Also small, but important, are emperor moths and bilberry bumblebees, both of which thrive here.

The bogs, bog pools and wet places, including the flushes that lead down from Pole Cottage and Shooting Box towards Lightspout Hollow, are full of exquisite mosses and sedges. The stream above Cow Ridge is one of the habitats of the upland golden-ringed dragonfly.

At Wildmoor Pool, there is bog bean and sundew, the county plant of Shropshire. Rushes and reeds shelter snipe and reed bunting. The patches of cotton grass that have appeared are indicators of landscape recovery.

The birds of the Mynd

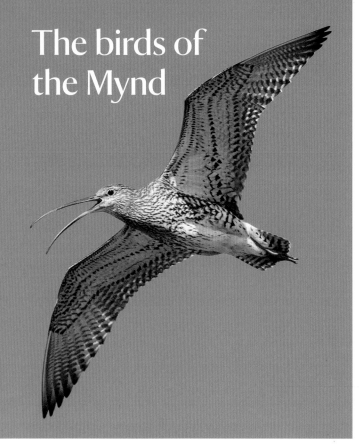

The Mynd is a haven for birdwatchers and photographers. There's always something to see, whatever the time of day or season. For the last three years I have been walking, crawling, stumbling, sitting very quietly or using my car as a hide and the heather as cover to get close to an array of species.

When whinchats and whitethroats mark their territories, I have heard their eloquent song and witnessed their beautiful markings, by going in softly and sitting in silence. The flushes that lead to Lightspout Hollow and down from Pole Cottage are good for bird spotting. Along with stonechats and reed buntings, ravens and hobbies have flown right past and grouse have posed by Pole Cottage in the last dregs of dusk.

Twitching hotspots

The grey wagtail has sung by the mosses of Lightspout Waterfall, where a pair nests most years, and the peregrine has persisted on the Mynd where elsewhere it is persecuted, poisoned and shot.

Curlews fly from the valleys to feed on the hilltops, and skylarks are everywhere among the heather as they vault overhead, spiralling into the sky.

There are wheatears in the spring and summer months, and it is worth slowing down to check the fencing and posts between Pole Cottage and the gliding station, where they like to perch.

Bramblings love the trees at Pole Cottage and golden plover can be seen at High Park in the winter.

For birds of prey like buzzard and kite, the sky is your first port of call, but also check perches such as rocky outcrops or singular hawthorn trees on slopes like Cow Ridge, where cuckoos can also be heard calling. Both merlins and peregrines breed on the Mynd, and hen harriers and short-eared owls are occasional visitors. There are plenty of kestrels all year round, which like to ride the west flank thermals, as do ravens, and inter-species aerial battles often break out.

The trees also play host to the much rarer cousin of the meadow pipit, the tree pipit. The bog pools behind Pole Cottage and Wildmoor Pool are reed-bunting territory.

The bird's-eye view on pages 28–29 is a good guide to the where and when of birds on the Mynd.

Above, left to right
A curlew in a blue sky; a raven landing; a hobby in flight; a grey wagtail

Left A whitethroat singing

The Mynd in all seasons

The Long Mynd is a backdrop for all that the seasons can offer. The hills and valleys are a year-round offering: from bracing winter walks and the birdsong of spring, to the hot days of summer with a haze of purple heather; autumn ushers in a new palette of colours sometimes shrouded in mist.

In spring the Long Mynd bursts into life. Migrant birds return and the wet flushes fill with the song of stonechat and whinchat. Cuckoos call from the valleys and lone, ancient hawthorns fill with white blossom. There is a choir of sound and song, from the ravens croaking as they carry nest-building twigs, to the cry of the red kite. Skylarks can be heard again, particularly around the road that passes the gliding station. Their song is an affirmation that winter has lost its grip.

Summer brings heat and thundery storms. To walk or cycle the Mynd under deep blue skies is a delight, especially with plenty of streams to cool tired feet, or the Carding Mill Valley reservoir if you're up for a chilly plunge. When the heather flowers in August, it's a celebration of both colour and landscape recovery. The purple has an intensity about it. This is a time for contemplation, picnics and photography. Most birds have finished breeding but the grouse are still about and hawks are on the wing. Hobbies fly over in search of dragonflies. The golden-ringed dragonfly can be spotted, laying her eggs in stream and pool, where the larvae can live up to five years before emerging into new-winged life. There are also butterflies – graylings, green hairstreaks, small coppers and small heaths.

Autumn is my favourite season, when the clouds appear to fall onto the earth. On cold clear nights, it's worth rising early to catch the Mynd and all its views at dawn. The inverted mists fill the valleys in the early morning before the sun rises to burn the fog away. Here is a time of burnishing as the last of the heather, the leaves, the trees, all move toward the gold that sums up this time of year. A few late dragonflies hover over the bog pools and kestrel hunt the high slopes, waiting for a field vole to dart from cover.

Winter is to be watched. Dawn and dusk fill with impossible reds and oranges, rich with the clarity of cold, frosty weather. Sometimes you can have the whole Mynd to yourself. When the wind flies in, it's best to be prepared, as conditions can turn arctic. Beware! The main access roads are closed on the coldest days for a reason, as black ice is a danger no car can overcome on the steepest way. But with determination and good walking boots, a snowy adventure is possible and then the Mynd can reveal incredible gifts of frozen bog pools and white, bare-tree wastes.

Far left A stonechat in a spring shower

Above Heather in summer

Above right Inverted mist on an autumnal dawn

Left Hawthorn on a snowy slope

Best for bird-spotting

All year round the valley sides and flushes are good places to spot stonechat and peregrine. In spring they might be joined by whinchat, redstart, merlin, curlew and cuckoo. Cuckoos, more often heard than seen, stay for the summer. Here are some other choice birdwatching spots, with what you might hope to see through the seasons.

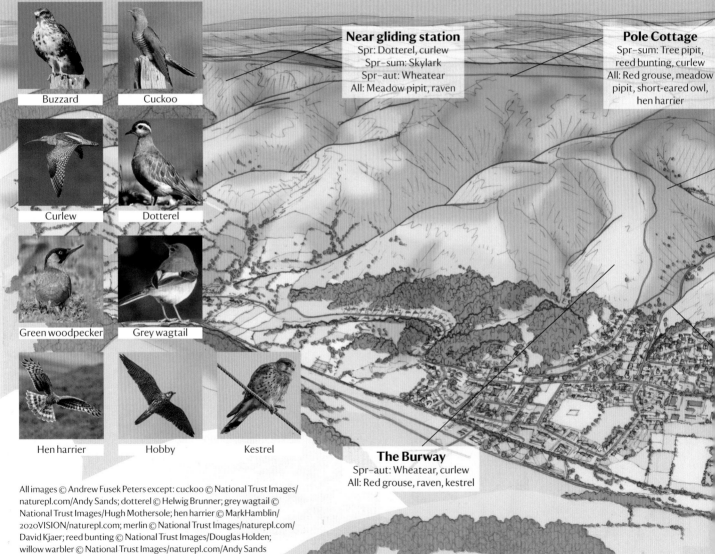

Buzzard

Cuckoo

Curlew

Dotterel

Green woodpecker

Grey wagtail

Hen harrier

Hobby

Kestrel

Near gliding station
Spr: Dotterel, curlew
Spr–sum: Skylark
Spr–aut: Wheatear
All: Meadow pipit, raven

Pole Cottage
Spr–sum: Tree pipit, reed bunting, curlew
All: Red grouse, meadow pipit, short-eared owl, hen harrier

The Burway
Spr–aut: Wheatear, curlew
All: Red grouse, raven, kestrel

All images © Andrew Fusek Peters except: cuckoo © National Trust Images/naturepl.com/Andy Sands; dotterel © Helwig Brunner; grey wagtail © National Trust Images/Hugh Mothersole; hen harrier © Mark Hamblin/2020VISION/naturepl.com; merlin © National Trust Images/naturepl.com/David Kjaer; reed bunting © National Trust Images/Douglas Holden; willow warbler © National Trust Images/naturepl.com/Andy Sands

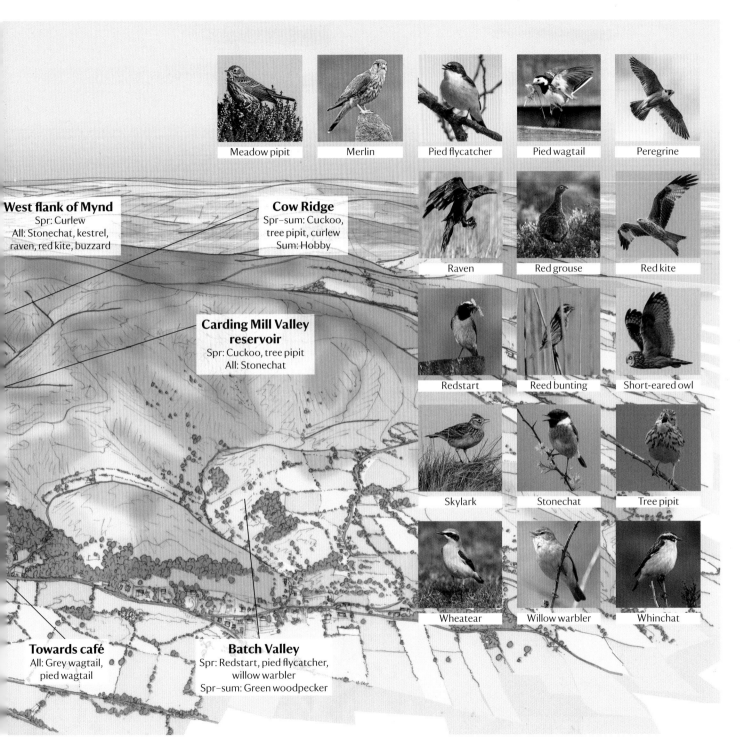

Meadow pipit

Merlin

Pied flycatcher

Pied wagtail

Peregrine

Raven

Red grouse

Red kite

Redstart

Reed bunting

Short-eared owl

Skylark

Stonechat

Tree pipit

Wheatear

Willow warbler

Whinchat

West flank of Mynd
Spr: Curlew
All: Stonechat, kestrel,
raven, red kite, buzzard

Cow Ridge
Spr-sum: Cuckoo,
tree pipit, curlew
Sum: Hobby

**Carding Mill Valley
reservoir**
Spr: Cuckoo, tree pipit
All: Stonechat

Towards café
All: Grey wagtail,
pied wagtail

Batch Valley
Spr: Redstart, pied flycatcher,
willow warbler
Spr-sum: Green woodpecker

Getting starry-eyed

The Long Mynd is a dedicated Dark Sky Discovery Site and the perfect place to bring your eyes, camera or telescope and stare at the heavens above on a clear night.

There are four official sites with the category 'Milky Way Class' – Shooting Box, Pole Cottage, Cross Dyke (wheelchair accessible) and Carding Mill Valley. The best nights to view the Milky Way are when there is a new moon, or if the moon is late rising or already set. The moon is incredibly bright, and if you wish to see the Milky Way clearly or photograph it, moonshine will affect the outcome.

However, it is worth spending some time on the Mynd and finding your own spot to take in the night sky. The bog pools behind Pole Cottage on a clear, windless night can catch reflections and Wildmoor Pool, where I took this photo, springs to life with a long exposure, even some considerable time after the end of astronomical twilight. Although the Mynd is a Dark Sky Discovery Site, there is still, sadly, a fair amount of light pollution. In this picture, what resembles a sunset is in fact light emanating from the streets of a town some distance away. There are few places to escape this, unless you dip into Carding Mill Valley where the hills block out town light. But the Mynd does offer a chance to look up and explore a different kind of landscape.

What the Mynd means to me

The Mynd has been a good neighbour all my adult life and it never ceases to amaze me. In a short drive, up past Asterton, or climbing the Burway, delving into Long Batch or the far reaches of High Park and over to Ratlinghope, it always feels like a new, strange country. For photographers there is so much to do, you could never dare to be bored.

I began my photographic journey focusing on wildlife. The first time I caught the elusive grouse, commuting across the road by Pole Cottage at 7am one summer dawn, I was ecstatic. But these smaller frames lived in a larger context, and I began to chase the light of dawn and dusk, understanding that they were as hard to catch as a hobby or a hen harrier.

Above A forest of foxgloves

Below My first grouse

Right In conversation with a stonechat

The Mynd always surprises. On its western flank above the road near Myndtown, there is another summer flowering that gives fair competition to the swathes of purple heather. Stands of foxgloves indicate a long-ago forest. These are not small clusters, but acres of swaying vibrancy.

Within this forest, one bird in particular sets out his stall. I crawled quietly to within a few feet of the single foxglove from which this bird liked to sing. I waited, and the stonechat returned, tiny claws gripping enfolded buds, both of us eyeing each other, as once again I came to a place not knowing what to look for or expect, but finding this. For life through the lens, I cannot recommend the Mynd highly enough.